Ancient Rome

ISBN 1-74089-366-2
Colour reproduction by
Colourscan Overseas Co Pte Ltd
Printed by SNP Leefung Printers

Printed in China

Ancient Rome

CONSULTING EDITOR

Dr Paul C. Roberts
Curator of Roman Archaeology
Department of Greek and Roman Antiquities
British Museum, London

WELDON OWEN

Contents

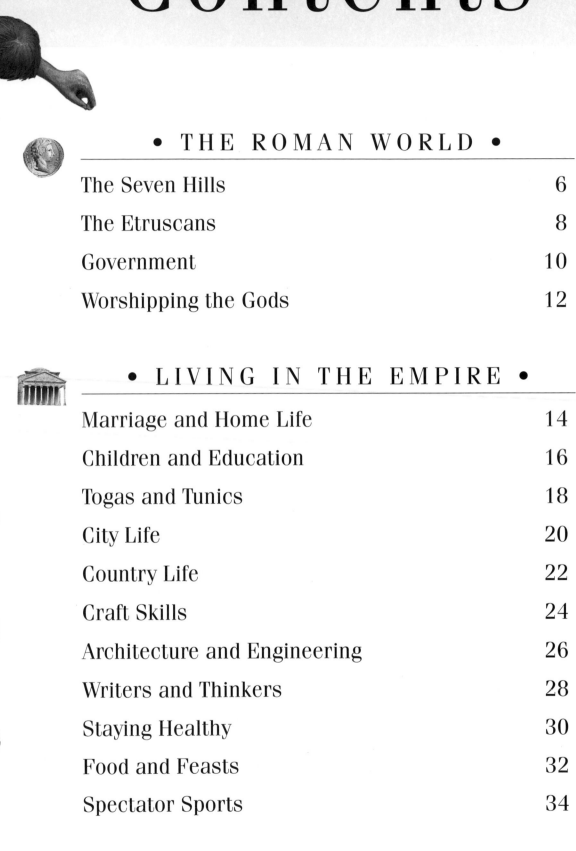

• EXPANSION AND EMPIRE •

• THE FALL OF ROME •

The Seven Hills

In ancient times, Rome covered seven hills overlooking the River Tiber. Nobody knows for sure who founded Rome, but one legend tells that twin brothers, Romulus and Remus, began building the city in 753 BC. Their mother, Rhea Silvia, was descended from Aeneas, a prince of Troy. Their father was Mars, the god of war. Romulus became Rome's first king after he killed his brother in a quarrel. Archaeologists know from artefacts they have found that from the eighth century BC farming communities were scattered across the seven hills. Gradually, they joined together to form Rome. The city grew strong and rich. It was first ruled by kings, then set up as a republic governed by the people, and finally controlled by a long line of emperors. The eagle became the symbol of the Empire and was carried into battle by Roman soldiers. The army conquered many lands. At its most successful, the Roman Empire circled the Mediterranean and Black seas and stretched north as far as Hadrian's Wall in Britain.

BRITANNIA
London

GAUL

Marseilles

HISPANIA

AFRICA

ROMAN LEGEND
Rhea Silvia's jealous uncle ordered that Romulus and Remus should be drowned in the River Tiber. A she-wolf discovered the babies and fed them with her milk.

THE PORT OF ROME
Ostia, at the mouth of the River Tiber, is about 25 km (15.5 miles) by road from the city of Rome. This coin shows ships in Ostia's ancient harbour.

753 BC	753–510 BC	510–27 BC	27 BC	AD 395	AD 476	AD 1453
The legendary date for the founding of Rome.	Rome is ruled by a series of kings.	The Roman Republic.	The Roman Empire is established under Augustus, the first emperor.	The Empire is split into West and East.	The Western Empire collapses.	The last city of the Eastern (Byzantine) Roman Empire is captured.

DACIA

GERMANIA

BLACK SEA

Ravenna

Constantinople

MACEDONIA

ASIA

RSICA

Rome

Ostia

ADRIATIC SEA

SYRIA

Pompeii

ACHAEA

CYPRUS

SARDINIA

Athens

Damascus

IONIAN SEA

AEGEAN SEA

SICILIA

CRETA

Jerusalem

Carthage

MEDITERRANEAN SEA

JUDAEA

Alexandria

AEGYPTUS

DID YOU KNOW?

"Italos" was the Greek word for bull-calf. Because the earliest Romans used cattle as a form of money, this "land of calves" soon became known as Italy.

Discover more in Empire in Decline

7

MYTHICAL BEAST
The Etruscans adopted some figures from Greek mythology, such as this lion-like monster called a chimaera. It has a goat's head in the middle of its back and a serpent for a tail.

BANQUETING IN STYLE
Large wall paintings in Etruscan tombs, which were sealed off from the air for about 2,500 years, have lasted amazingly well. Scenes, such as this one of people at a sumptuous banquet, show how much the Etruscans enjoyed themselves.

The Etruscans

GUARDIAN OF THE GATE
This two-faced god is looking forwards and backwards in time. He may be an earlier Etruscan version of Janus, the Roman god of exits and entrances.

People lived in Italy long before Rome was built. There were Latins, Samnites, Umbrians, Sabines, Greeks and the most powerful of all—the Etruscans. They occupied Etruria, which spread to the north and south of Rome. Etruria had a good climate, rich soil for farming, rocks containing useful metal ores, and thick forests to provide wood for building houses, temples, boats and bridges. One story suggests that the Etruscans came to Italy from Lydia in Asia Minor when food was scarce in their own country. Archaeologists cannot prove this, but they know a great deal about Etruscan daily life and their well-planned cities from what these early settlers buried in their tombs. They furnished the underground tombs like their homes with many fine bronze and terracotta clay statues. The Etruscans excelled at making music, and raising and riding horses. They were also skilled engineers. At times Etruscan kings ruled Rome, and the Etruscans and Latins later became one group of people.

MODELLED IN TERRACOTTA
In the ancient world, men and women usually dined separately. In Etruria, however, husbands and wives often feasted together, as shown on the lid of this coffin.

Did You Know?
The Etruscans made colours for their paintings from rocks and minerals. Crushed chalk gave them white, powdered charcoal made black, and oxidised iron granules made red.

ON GUARD
Etruscan sculptors made many statues from bronze. They often portrayed warriors with huge, crested helmets, which made the soldiers look taller and thinner.

Telling the Future
The Etruscans worshipped many gods. Priests, called augurs, claimed they could tell what the gods wanted from certain natural signs. They read meaning into thunder, lightning, and the flight of birds, and told the future from the insides of dead animals, especially the liver. This replica of a sheep's liver (left) is marked out in sections, each with the name of a different god. It was possibly used by augurs when examining a liver, as shown on the back of the mirror above.

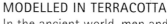
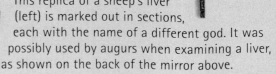

Government

Kings ruled Rome until 510 BC when the citizens expelled the last king, Tarquin the Proud. Rome then became a republic governed by officials who were elected by the people. Each year, the citizens chose two consuls and other government administrators from a group called the Senate. The idea was to prevent any one man from having too much power. Julius Caesar (above left), a brilliant general, had many military successes, which helped him to gain popularity and power in the Republic. In 49 BC, he marched his army to Rome and seized power. A civil war followed in which Caesar defeated his rivals and became the ruler of Rome. This one-man rule worried some senators and Caesar was murdered in 44 BC. His death brought renewed civil war and the collapse of the Republic. Caesar's adopted son Octavian gained control and brought peace to the Roman world. Octavian was renamed Augustus, and in 27 BC he became the first of Rome's many emperors. Some emperors, such as Augustus and Trajan, governed well. Others, such as Domitian and Nero, used their power badly.

CITY CENTRE
The heart of every Roman town and city was the forum. This open square was surrounded by government buildings and temples. People came to the forum to vote, hear speeches, attend the law courts, read public notices and discuss the issues of the day.

DID YOU KNOW?
Roman emperors did not wear crowns like kings. Instead, they wore laurel wreaths on their heads. These had once been given to generals to celebrate victories in battle.

SYMBOL OF LAW
The fasces was a bundle of rods and an axe that symbolised the power of a magistrate. It was carried for him by his young attendant. The Romans took this symbol from the Etruscans.

HONOURING AUGUSTUS
The marble Altar of Augustan Peace in Rome is carved on all sides with subjects that reflect the greatness of Rome's first emperor, Augustus. This panel shows members of the imperial family.

FACES IN STONE
Carved pictures in layered stone, called cameos, often portrayed important people. This one shows the emperor Claudius, his wife Agrippina the Younger, and her relatives.

THE SOCIAL ORDER

The people of ancient Rome were either citizens or non-citizens. Citizens were divided into three levels: wealthy patricians (such as the man shown here holding busts of his ancestors); businessmen called equites; and commoners called plebeians. At first, only patricians were allowed to be senators. Later, plebeians gained representation in the Senate, but the emperors took away this power. Non-citizens included women, slaves, foreigners and people who lived in the provinces.

Discover more in Growing Empire

11

• THE ROMAN WORLD •

Worshipping the Gods

The ancient Romans worshipped the same gods as the Greeks, but they gave them different names. The Greek god Zeus, for example, was called Jupiter, and the goddess Hera became Juno. People worshipped their gods through prayer, offerings of food and wine, and animal sacrifices. They also believed that natural things, such as trees and rivers, and objects that were made, such as doors, hinges and doorsteps, all had their own divine spirits. The head of the household was responsible for religious rituals in the home. Government officials performed religious duties in temples. Priests, called augurs, examined the insides of dead animals and looked for meaning in the flight of birds, which they believed were messengers from the gods. The expansion of the Empire introduced the Romans to new religions. These were permitted, provided worshippers did not ignore the Roman gods or threaten Roman government. The Jews and the Christians endured centuries of hardship because their beliefs challenged the emperors' authority.

RELIGION FROM EGYPT
The worship of Isis, the goddess of heaven and earth, first became fashionable in Rome after the Egyptian Queen Cleopatra spent a year there. Later, Isis had followers throughout the Empire.

HOUSEHOLD SHRINE
Every Roman house had an altar for the household gods. Here, spirits of the home, the larder and the family's special god (centre) stand above a sacred serpent.

WORSHIPPING BACCHUS
Followers of Dionysus sacrificed goats to him. This Greek god of wine and the theatre was known to the ancient Romans as Bacchus (right).

A PERSIAN GOD
Many Roman soldiers worshipped Mithras, the bull-slayer, god of light and wisdom. Mithras was supposed to have been born holding a sword.

A TEMPLE FOR AUGUSTUS
This temple at Nîmes, in what is now France, was built during the reign of the emperor Augustus. It was dedicated to the worship of the emperor.

THE VESTAL VIRGINS

Vesta, the goddess of the hearth, was worshipped in every household. Six priestesses, called Vestal Virgins, tended her state shrine in Rome's forum. They had to keep her sacred flame burning continuously. It was a great honour to be chosen as a Vestal Virgin.

THE GOD OF BEGINNINGS

Two-faced Janus, looking backwards and forwards, supposedly understood both the past and the future. Janus was the god of beginnings—such as the first hour of the day. The first month of the year, January, was named after him. This early Roman god of exits and entrances guarded doors, gateways and arches. The doors to his shrine in Rome were always open in times of war, but closed during peace.

INTERIOR DECORATION
The rooms in grand homes were built around courtyards and colonnades. Artists covered the inside walls with scenes painted on wet plaster. This picture is in a villa at Pompeii.

JOINING OF HANDS
A Roman bride wore a white tunic, a saffron-coloured veil and a wreath made from marjoram. The couple clasped right hands while the marriage contract was read and sealed. Later, the groom carried the bride over the threshold of her new home.

FACES FROM THE PAST
Roman couples often had their likenesses painted on wood or as frescoes on the walls of their houses. This portrait was found in a house at Pompeii.

AT PLAY
Rich women amused themselves by playing music. They often sat on high-backed bronze chairs, which were a sign of wealth. Most Romans sat on wooden stools.

• LIVING IN THE EMPIRE •

Marriage and Home Life

The father was head of the household. He was called the paterfamilias and he had complete power over his family and slaves. Although men legally controlled women, husbands often consulted their wives in private about public matters. Women were not entirely without rights, but they never became full citizens. Widows could own property, and some women became priestesses, shopkeepers, hairdressers, midwives or doctors. Highborn women employed slaves to raise the children, shop, clean and cook. Parents arranged marriages for their children. The wedding date was chosen carefully and the second half of July was considered a lucky time. A priest would study the insides of a dead animal looking for signs that would indicate good fortune for the couple. Girls married at about 14 and wore a metal wedding ring (above left) on the third finger of their left hand. A marriage was not final until a wife had stayed in her husband's home for a full year.

A Slave's Life

Thousands of prisoners from Greece, Egypt, North Africa, Britain and other conquered lands laboured as slaves in homes, fields, mines, workshops and on building projects. They were punished severely for work badly done or for running away, and some slaves had to wear identity tags (above) and collars (below). But not all were ill-treated. "Treat your slave with kindness" advised the philosopher Seneca. Many educated Greek slaves became teachers or doctors. Some slaves earned wages and saved to buy their freedom.

TIME TO CELEBRATE
This children's procession was held in Ostia. Processions were a way of celebrating religious festivals, battle victories and weddings.

WRITING ON WAX
This girl holds wooden tablets that are coated on one side with wax and tied together to form a type of notebook. She is writing with a bone stylus.

• LIVING IN THE EMPIRE •

Children and Education

Wealthy couples thought children were a blessing and hoped to have large families. But women often died in childbirth and many babies and small children did not survive because the Romans had little knowledge of hygiene and childhood diseases. Parents sometimes abandoned their sickly infants outside the city's walls. Poor people found children costly to raise and their offspring went to work at an early age without any schooling. There was no free education in ancient Rome, and when children were about six, those from wealthy families started school where fees had to be paid, or began lessons at home. Many families employed educated Greek slaves as tutors. At 11, some boys went to secondary schools where they learnt history, geography, geometry, astronomy, music and philosophy. At 14, boys who wanted a career in politics or law began to study public speaking. Girls learnt basic reading, writing and mathematics and how to run a home.

A BOY'S LIFE
This carving shows four stages in a boy's childhood: at his mother's breast, accepted by his father, riding in a toy chariot drawn by a donkey, and with his teacher.

A NEW BABY
A father held his newborn infant in his arms to show that he accepted his son or daughter. In a ceremony nine days after being born, the baby received a name and a neck charm, called a bulla, to ward off evil spirits.

16

LEARNING LESSONS
Schoolboys read their lessons from long papyrus scrolls. Papyrus came from Egypt where the plants grew plentifully beside the River Nile. Paper was made by beating the fibres of the stems.

THE TOGA OF MANHOOD

At the age of 14, boys were expected to behave as men. Every March, during the feast of the god Bacchus, special coming-of-age ceremonies for citizens' sons were held in the forum. The boys took off their neck charms (right), and exchanged their childhood clothing for adult togas. Barbers gave them their first shave and they were registered as citizens. The ceremonies ended with the boys making offerings of sacred honey cakes on the altar of Bacchus.

MOTHER AND CHILD
This gravestone in Palmyra, Syria is an early tribute to a mother and child. The theme is repeated in Christian paintings of Mary and Jesus.

SPRING BOUQUET
Here, Primavera, the goddess of spring, walks through the countryside gathering flowers. Her clothing, falling in soft folds, shows the elegance of fashionable female dress.

DRESSED FOR BEST
Fashions in clothing were slow to change in ancient Roman times. These two people are dressed in early Empire style. The woman is wearing a short tunic under a full-length one and has a long robe draped over the top. The man is clad in tunic and toga.

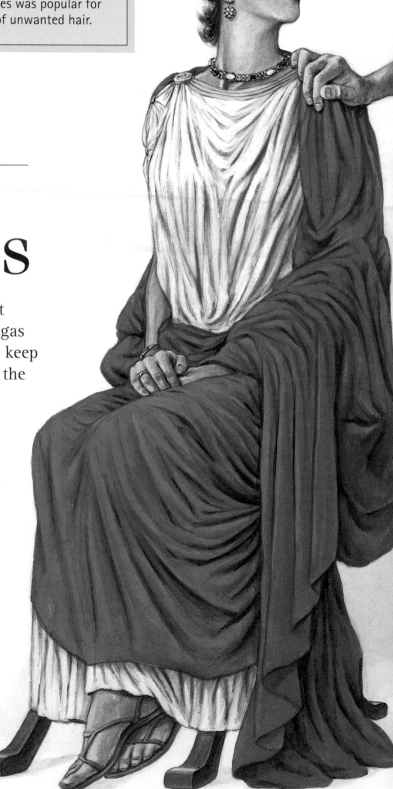

> ## DID YOU KNOW?
> Men went to special shops to have the hair on their arms removed. A mixture of bats' blood and hedgehog ashes was popular for getting rid of unwanted hair.

• LIVING IN THE EMPIRE •

Togas and Tunics

Togas, the dress of citizens, were first worn by the Etruscans. Although togas were uncomfortable and difficult to keep clean, these garments were popular with the emperors and remained fashionable for centuries. They were semicircular in shape and usually made from a single length of woollen cloth. The wearer held the heavy folds together as he moved, which left only the right arm free. Emperors wore purple togas; senators' togas were white and edged with a purple stripe. Citizens wore wool or linen tunics under their plain white togas, but other men, women and children wore tunics only. These were folded and pinned, and held with a belt. They seldom had stitched seams because sewing with thick bone or bronze needles was so difficult. During imperial times, wealthy people liked clothing made from finely woven Indian cotton and expensive Chinese silk. Jewellers crafted beautiful ornaments, such as gold earrings (above left). Women also wore jewellery made of polished amber from the cold Baltic countries, which was carved in the town of Aquileia in northeast Italy.

18

DELICATE JEWELLERY
Jewellers worked with many precious stones and metals imported from the provinces. This necklace is made from emeralds threaded on gold rods and joined with gold links.

IN FASHION
Beards went in and out of fashion through the centuries. In the second century AD, emperors such as Hadrian and Septimius Severus (right) led a trend towards beards.

SWEET PERFUMES
Women used great quantities of sweet-smelling oils. The most expensive came from Arabia and were bought in glass bottles, such as this one, from shops that specialised in perfumes and scented ointments.

HAIRSTYLES OF THE EMPIRE

Slaves spent hours dressing their mistresses' hair. They dyed and perfumed it, curled it with heated tongs, and coiled it into buns. Slaves who did a bad job could be beaten. Sometimes, dark-haired Roman ladies wore wigs made from blonde locks, or had hairpieces fixed in place with hairpins. Hairstyles changed often. Vibia Matidia, the emperor Trajan's niece (far right), and Faustina (right), wife of the emperor Marcus Aurelius, have two different imperial hairstyles.

Discover more in Food and Feasts

19

SEWER SYSTEMS
Sewers carried running water to private lavatories in wealthy homes and to public lavatories in the streets. In Rome, the waste ran into the River Tiber.

CITY SHOPPING
There were no supermarkets in Rome. Small shops specialised in particular goods. These relief carvings show a greengrocer (top) and a butcher (bottom).

City Life

Roman cities were laid out in a square with the main roads crossing at right angles. Buildings included a basilica that contained offices and law courts, temples, shops, workshops, public bathhouses and public lavatories. Aqueducts brought in water, while sewers removed waste. There was often a theatre for plays and an amphitheatre for other entertainments. Statues and decorated arches and columns were erected to commemorate important events. Cities were crowded and dirty. The rich had spacious town houses but most people lived in cramped conditions. Blocks of flats made of stone and wood were three to five storeys high. Sometimes they collapsed because they were so badly built. Most houses had no plumbing, and residents tipped waste down communal drains. Later, when the city of Rome became extremely overcrowded, the emperor passed a law forbidding people to move wheeled vehicles in daylight, so carts clattered after dark. The poet Martial complained, "there's nowhere a poor man can get any quiet in Rome".

STREET SCENE
Rome's narrow side streets were lined with stalls and shops. At night, the shopkeepers secured their goods behind heavy wooden shutters. Walls were covered with signs and advertisements. Some people carried their wares while others used donkeys to transport their goods.

TAKEAWAY SHOP
Most apartments had no kitchens. Hot food was sold from shops (right) and stalls, and many people cooked in the street using portable stoves.

IN MEMORIAM

Ancient Romans cremated or buried the dead, and believed that their spirits crossed the mythical River Styx to the Underworld (Hades). A coin placed in the dead person's mouth paid the ferryboat fare. Mourners and musicians accompanied the body through the streets to the cemetery outside the city's walls. Many monuments to the dead survive. The one above presents portraits of two freed slaves surrounded by the rods and staffs of the freedom ceremony (left), metalworker's tools (top) and carpenter's tools (right).

DID YOU KNOW?

City dwellers greatly feared fires. These were easily started by candles, oil lamps and portable stoves. Rome had seven fire brigades, equipped with hand pumps, buckets, hooks and axes, but they seldom managed to save houses that caught fire.

IMPERIAL GRANDEUR

The emperor Hadrian's villa at Tibur (now called Tivoli), near Rome, was set in a beautifully landscaped garden. Greek sculptures stood beside the many lakes and waterways.

COUNTRY ART

People spent a great deal of money on their country villas. Wall paintings, such as this one, sculptures and mosaics were just as elaborate as the art that decorated town houses.

Country Life

Throughout Italy and the provinces, large farming estates produced food for city dwellers and the army. Provinces such as Egypt and North Africa grew grain, Spain was famous for olive oil, Italy made the best wines, and Britain supplied beer and woollen goods. Farm slaves toiled from dawn to dusk, and were frequently whipped by the overseers who supervised them in the fields. Oxen and cattle pulled ploughs, and donkeys and mules were used for other work. The famous Roman poet Virgil wrote a practical handbook for farmers in the form of a poem called the *Georgics*. In it, he advised them to "enrich the dried-up soil with dung", and told them how to rotate crops and keep corn free of weeds. The crops grown depended largely on soil and climate. In Italy, farmers grew grapes, olives and many vegetables. Pork was a favourite meat and large numbers of pigs were raised. Sheep and goats were kept for wool and milk. Farmers also raised chickens, ducks, geese and pigeons, and kept bees for their honey.

DID YOU KNOW?

In the fourth century AD, St Augustine wrote about the number of spirit gods worshipped by country people. At least 12 gods were linked to the growing of crops. Silvanus, for example, was the spirit of the boundary between cultivated fields and woodland.

COUNTRY HOLIDAY

Wealthy Romans owned luxurious houses in the country. Set among the estate's ploughed fields, orchards and livestock barns, the "villa urbana" had all the comforts of the owner's town dwelling. The part of the estate that housed the farm staff was called the "villa rustica".

GARDEN FRESCO

Livia, wife of the emperor Augustus, had a villa at Primaporta outside Rome. This fresco on the wall of one of the small rooms created a cool feeling during summer.

FARMING IN THE EMPIRE

By imperial times, much land had been organised into large estates and small farms were unusual. Wealthy landowners, living mostly in town, employed farm managers and slaves. Farming methods changed little over the centuries. Oxen pulled ploughs or pushed threshing machines. Farm workers wielded iron hoes, rakes, scythes and sickles, and trod the juice from grapes. In later times, Roman engineers invented waterwheels to grind corn. These saved much time and energy.

MAKING MOSAICS
Mosaicists used hammers and chisels to cut sandstone and marble into small coloured cubes called tesserae. Working over a pattern or picture, they pressed the tesserae and pieces of glass into a bedding of soft mortar. Finally, they cleaned and polished the surface thoroughly.

DID YOU KNOW?
Pottery was traded across the Empire. Scientists can now find out where the clay came from originally by examining tiny pieces under powerful microscopes, or by chemical analysis of fragments.

DANCING FAUN
This bronze faun, a country god, stood in the courtyard of a house in Pompeii. Like so many other Roman statues, it was copied from a Greek sculpture.

RESTING EMPRES'
A full-length marble statue was a common form of portrait for important people during imperial times. This is Agrippina, wife of the emperor Claudit

Craft Skills

In small workshops behind city shops, craftworkers turned metal, clay, stone, glass, wood, animal bones, ivory, cloth, leather and other materials into useful and decorative objects. Potteries in Gaul (present-day France), Italy and North Africa produced great numbers of red pots, which were exported all over the Empire. Fresco painters, stonemasons, mosaicists and carpenters worked at people's houses or on public buildings, which were often commissioned by the emperors. Cameo carving (the art of making pictures from layered stone) and mosaic (the art of making designs from small pieces of coloured stone and glass) were both popular during the time of the Empire. Cameo carvers usually worked with sardonyx, a semiprecious stone that formed naturally in layers of different colours. In the centuries before the Empire, generations of Roman craftworkers learnt from Etruscan art and from Greek pottery, painting and sculpture. They copied Greek statues and the technique of carving friezes in stone. Craftworkers passed on their skills to their sons.

CARVED GLASS

The dark inner layer of this glass vase was encased in opaque white glass, which was then skilfully cut away to produce the decoration.

DRINKING CUPS

Silver cups survive from the first century BC. This one features a scene from a Greek tragedy by Sophocles.

DRINKING DOVES

This mosaic, made from thousands of tesserae, decorated the emperor Hadrian's villa. The Roman artist copied a Greek original.

BLOWING GLASS

Glass-blowing, which was developed in the first century BC, was an important technological breakthrough. Glass-blowing probably began in Syria, but it spread quickly across the West. Glass workshops were hot and uncomfortable, but this new technique allowed skilled craftworkers to make objects in many shapes. Sometimes they combined old moulding methods with blowing. Glass became a cheap, everyday material and most people throughout the Empire could afford some glassware.

Discover more in The Etruscans

25

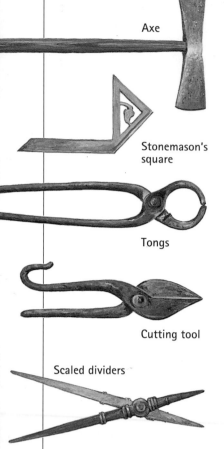

Axe

Stonemason's square

Tongs

Cutting tool

Scaled dividers

BUILDERS' TOOLS
Most Roman tools were made from iron and some had wooden handles. The tools above are a similar shape to modern tools.

Architecture and Engineering

For centuries, Roman architects were content to adapt Greek styles to suit their own tastes. They also adopted the arch from Mesopotamia. Arches spread the weight of a load and were used in bridges, aqueducts and amphitheatres. In the second century BC, the Romans developed concrete, a mixture of volcanic ash, lime and water that set as hard as rock. Concrete made it possible to build large, strong, domed roofs, such as the one on the Pantheon in Rome. Engineers used a tool called a groma to check that buildings and roads were straight. They worked out efficient water systems and invented waterwheels to drive flour mills. Many emperors organised building programs. Augustus boasted that he found Rome a city of brick and left it a city of marble. Vespasian was responsible for building Rome's great amphitheatre, the Colosseum, and Trajan ordered the construction of a towering victory column. Hadrian's many building successes included his luxury villa at Tivoli and a frontier wall in northern Britain.

OLIVE PRESS
Olive presses operated on a screw thread, a clever device that made turning easier. The oil was crushed from the fruit under the block at the base.

PANTHEON OF GODS
Rome's Pantheon, built mainly during Hadrian's reign, honoured all the state gods and still stands. Its domed roof, the largest of its time, represented the heavens; the circular opening stood for the sun. People offered gifts to the gods at altars inside this magnificent building.

METAL FORGE
A metalworker (centre) holds the hot metal in tongs while he beats it into shape. More metalworkers' tools can be seen on the right of this relief carving.

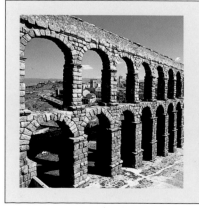

WATER SUPPLIES

Imperial cities had fresh water supplies. At one time, 11 great aqueducts fed Rome's bathhouses, fountains and public lavatories. Some of them were linked with springs 48 km (30 miles) away. The water flowed gently from a higher level to a lower one. Arches, in one, two or three tiers, supported the pipes across steep valleys. Tunnels took them through hills. Invading barbarian tribes destroyed many Roman aqueducts, but ruins like the ones at Segovia in Spain (left) show us what they were like.

DID YOU KNOW?
Not all slaves were owned by
individuals. Some belonged to towns.
These slaves led miserable lives,
labouring in chain gangs on road
works and other engineering projects.

LIVING IN THE EMPIRE

Writers and Thinkers

Latin was the official language of business and trade in the empire in the West, while Greek was used in the empire in the East. People in the provinces spoke local tongues. Latin, which had an alphabet of 22 letters, was inscribed on stone or wax tablets, or written in ink (inkpots above left) on papyrus scrolls, pieces of wood, or thin animal skins called vellum. Only educated Romans could read and write. After they conquered ancient Greece, the Romans' admiration for Greek literature and ideas increased. Homer's Greek *Odyssey* inspired Virgil to write the *Aeneid*. Horace, Ovid and Martial also produced fine poetry. Some historians, including Livy, Pliny the Elder and Tacitus, recorded the events of the day. Two Greek philosophies, Epicureanism and Stoicism, attracted Roman followers. Epicureans believed that a person's happiness depended on pleasure and avoiding pain. Stoics believed that happiness came from thinking things through carefully and not giving way to your feelings.

PTOLEMAIC MAP
Ptolemy, c.AD 90 to c.168, was a mathematician, astronomer and geographer who had a lasting influence on Western scientists. This map of the world, drawn in 1540, is based on his ideas.

LITERARY MASTERPIECE
Here Virgil sits between the Muses of epic poetry and tragedy. His long poem the *Aeneid* describes the adventures of the Trojan prince Aeneas and how he came to the land of the Latins.

EYEWITNESS
Pliny the Younger, a Roman writer, watched with his aunt as Mt Vesuvius erupted in AD 79. His uncle Pliny the Elder died from the fumes. Pliny the Younger later recorded what he saw. He also travelled widely, and his letters to his friend Tacitus and to the emperor Trajan tell us much about life at this time.

ROMAN NUMERALS
The letters I, V and X represent the numbers 1, 5 and 10. If "I" is before a letter, it is subtracted from it. IV stands for 4. If "I" comes after a letter, it is added to it. VI represents 6.

THE JULIAN CALENDAR

In 46 BC, Julius Caesar established the calendar that became accepted throughout the Roman Empire. It was devised by the mathematician Sosigenes. In order to make it work, 67 days were added in 45 BC. The new calendar gave the year 365 days, which were divided into 12 months. Seven months had 31 days, four had 30 days and one had 28 days, as does the modern Western calendar. An extra day was added every four years. The Romans worked for seven days. Every eighth day was market day.

DAILY EXERCISE
Some young women exercised daily in the gymnasiums to keep trim. The ancient Romans believed that a healthy body ensured a healthy mind.

THE ORDER OF BATHING
Bathers began in a warm room with a pool filled with tepid water. Next, they moved to the steam room where the water was very hot. Finally, they plunged into cold water to cool off. Slaves attended to bathers' needs, cleaned the baths and stoked the furnaces.

• LIVING IN THE EMPIRE •

Staying Healthy

Diseases such as typhoid, dysentery and tuberculosis killed many people in the Empire's overcrowded cities, but minor ailments could also be serious. Cures were often unsuccessful because doctors did not understand the causes of illness. Treatments depended on basic scientific knowledge combined with folklore and prayer. The Empire's only hospitals were reserved for wounded soldiers. Every town had at least one public bathhouse, and cities often had several. Entrance fees were low for both men and women; children were admitted free. In Rome, besides baths, these huge complexes contained gymnasiums, massage rooms, takeaway food shops, libraries, and gardens where citizens met to exchange gossip and news. The emperors Titus, Trajan, Caracalla and Diocletian all sponsored the building of public bathhouses. The Baths of Caracalla could take 1,600 bathers a day. Tooth decay was not a serious problem for ancient Romans because they had no sugar in their diet. Honey was expensive and used sparingly.

BODY OIL
This oil flask and tools, called strigils, once belonged to a Roman athlete. Athletes oiled their bodies before exercising and scraped themselves clean afterwards.

HEALING WATER
The baths at Bath in England are filled with water from natural hot springs. These were sacred to the ancient Romans and used for healing purposes.

MEDICAL MATTERS

Many doctors practising in ancient Rome were Greek slaves or freedmen. They advised their patients on exercise and diet, prescribed herbal remedies that could be bought in chemists' shops (above) and did basic operations (instruments below). Sick people also appealed to magic and the gods, particularly to Asclepius, the god of healing. Patients who slept in his temples expected him to appear in their dreams with miraculous cures. Surgery was performed without anaesthetics and women often died during childbirth.

31

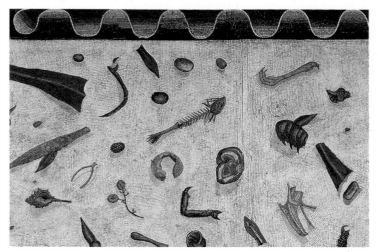

FOOD SCRAPS
This mosaic on a dining-room floor cleverly copies the debris from dinner. Guests would discard wishbones, fishbones, shells, lobsters' claws and fruit stones during the meal.

BANQUET BEHAVIOUR
Men and women ate together at Roman banquets. Guests dressed in their best clothing, but removed their shoes once inside the host's house. Diners reclined three to a couch and ate mostly with their fingers. They drank wine mixed with water.

BIRDS FOR DINNER
Artists studied animals carefully and reproduced their behaviour in accurate detail. In this mosaic, a cat is about to dine on a plump bird.

COOKING POTS
Cooking pots had to be strong because they were used frequently. Large pans (top centre) rested on iron grids above hot coals.

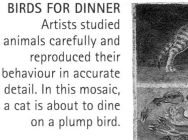

SERVING BOY
The children of slaves also became slaves. The luckier ones worked indoors in private homes and helped to prepare food.

Food and Feasts

Romans ate their main meal of the day late in the afternoon. Lower classes had wheat and barley porridge, bread, vegetables, olives and grapes, and made cheap cuts of meat into sausages, rissoles and pies. Emperors arranged for hand-outs of grain and oil to the very poor. If grain deliveries were delayed, riots sometimes broke out in Rome. The emperor Tiberius warned the Senate that stopping the corn dole would mean "the utter ruin of the state". Unlike the poor, wealthy citizens ate extremely well. There was a saying in imperial Rome that the rich fell ill from overeating and the poor from not eating enough. Slaves from the East, who were skilled in preparing exotic dishes, were in great demand as cooks. Hosts spent huge sums of money on food for a banquet, which might last well into the night. The meal had three courses, each consisting of a range of dishes served on pottery, glass or even silver or gold platters.

COOKING WITHOUT TOMATOES
There were many imported foods at banquets. But tomatoes did not reach Italy until the sixteenth century, after they were discovered in the Americas.

BANQUET DISHES

Roman cookery books listed dishes that required hours of preparation. Fish sauce, made from sprats, fish intestines, olive oil and herbs, was fermented in the sun for three days. Cooks might prepare appetisers of sows' udders or jellyfish stuffed with salted sea urchins. Main courses could include flamingo with dates, roast parrot, boiled ostrich, and dormice stuffed with pork and pine kernels. Romans liked fruit for dessert and army generals competed with one another to bring back new fruits from the provinces.

These terracotta figurines are models of gladiators. Although they are wearing Thracian helmets, the rest of their scanty clothing leaves parts of their body dangerously exposed.

THE NET MAN
Unlike other gladiators, who wore some protective armour, the almost naked retiarius carried only a weighted net, a Neptune's trident used by tuna fishermen and a short sword.

THE ROAR OF THE CROWD
Several pairs of gladiators might fight at the same time: Samnite against Samnite (below), armed with spear, sword and shield; Thracian against Samnite (centre); and retiarius against Samnite (right). The audience cheered winners and booed losers loudly.

• LIVING IN THE EMPIRE •

Spectator Sports

Emperors and provincial governors arranged chariot races and violent games to amuse people on the frequent public holidays. People of all classes flocked eagerly to these entertainments. Rome's Circus Maximus was always packed on race days, when chariots thundered round the track to the deafening noise made by 260,000 onlookers. Most charioteers were slaves and the successful ones earned freedom. Convicts and slaves (both men and women) trained as gladiators. Equipped in the styles of warriors, such as Samnites and Thracians, or armed with fishing gear, they fought each other and wild animals, while musicians played bronze horns and water organs. Rome's amphitheatre, known as the Colosseum, seated 60,000 spectators. The contestants shouted, "We who are about to die, salute you!" as they filed past the imperial stand during opening parades. Wounded gladiators could appeal for mercy, but jeers from the crowd and the thumbs-down signal brought death from the referee. Victorious gladiators were treated as stars and won their freedom.

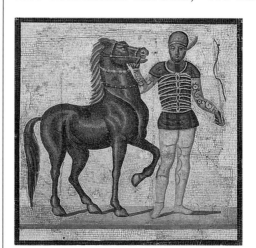

CHARIOTEERS' COLOURS
In Rome, there were four important chariot teams—Reds, Blues, Whites and Greens (above). Every team had a large group of fans. Sometimes fights broke out between the different groups.

DID YOU KNOW?
One of the games staged in Rome on orders from the emperor Trajan lasted for 117 days. More than 10,000 gladiators took part.

FIRST PAST THE POST
Chariots were drawn by teams of two, three or four horses (left). Charioteers fell frequently during the race. First place went to the winning chariot, either with or without a driver.

GOING TO THE THEATRE

Roman plays, which at first were translations from the Greek, included tragedies and comedies. Like the Greeks, Roman dramatic actors were male and wore masks (above). The audiences, who voiced their opinions noisily, preferred comedies. The most famous comedies were written by Plautus and Terence. The Romans developed comic mimes, which were performed without masks or words on rough stages in the streets. Women acted in these mimes. Because large-scale dramas were not as popular as other entertainments, some of the huge stone theatres later became gladiatorial arenas.

HARBOUR SCENE
The Romans built deep harbours like this one, which is probably in the Bay of Naples, so that goods and passengers could be loaded and unloaded safely onto ships.

Roads and Travel

Roman roads, constructed by the army and slave labourers, carried soldiers, messengers, travellers and traders across the Empire. These straight, level highways followed the most direct routes, tunnelling through hills and bridging rivers. They formed a network that allowed troops to march quickly to any trouble spot, and connected towns, cities and ports with Rome, the capital and centre of government. Road construction usually began with digging a ditch about 1 m (3 ft) deep. This was filled with sand, and then with small stones and gravel mixed with concrete. Paving stones were laid on top and milestones set in place to mark distances. Roman roads were crammed with all kinds of people and animals. The rich travelled in carriages with several slaves. They sometimes slept in their vehicles or in tents pitched by the roadside because they were frightened of being robbed at the inns. Some roads lasted for many centuries and many present-day European roads follow old Roman routes.

MEASURED BY MILESTONES
Inscriptions in Roman numbers on low pillars of stone, placed at the edges of roads, told travellers the distances between towns.

DID YOU KNOW?
Road transport was slow and therefore expensive. Horses were faster than bullocks, but the Romans had no harnesses that allowed horses to pull heavy wagons. Horses were ridden or used to pull light carts.

HIGHWAY ONE

The first Roman road, built in 312 BC, linked Rome to Capua in southern Italy. It was called the Via Appia and later extended even farther south to present-day Brindisi.

TOURING THE EMPIRE

Many Roman tourists visited the Seven Wonders of the World, such as the Egyptian pyramids at Giza (left), and other places in the Empire. There were even some maps and guidebooks available. A few sightseers left lasting evidence of their travels in Latin graffiti on stone monuments in Egypt. Travellers often asked soothsayers to read the future before they began what might be a dangerous adventure. Robbers ambushed tourists on Italian roads, and barbarians attacked them in foreign lands. Sea voyagers ran into pirates and foul weather.

ROADSIDE INNS

During long journeys travellers often stopped to eat and sleep at inns beside the road. Surviving accounts of people's journeys tell us that these inns frequently served poor food and bad water. The noisy behaviour of some of the guests often kept others awake.

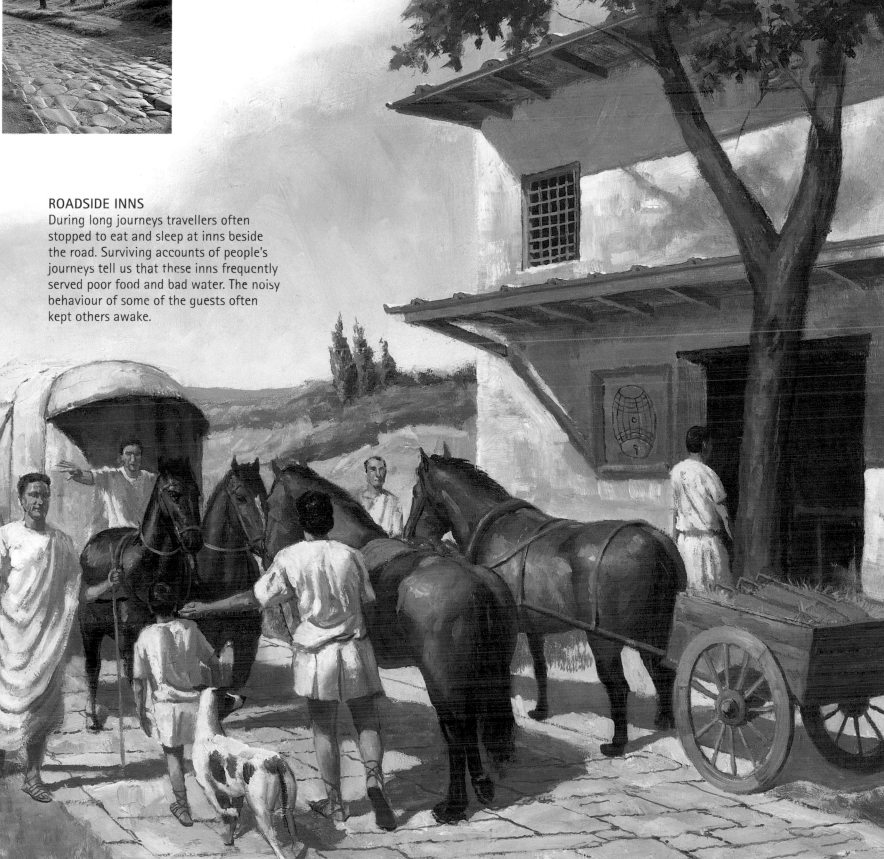

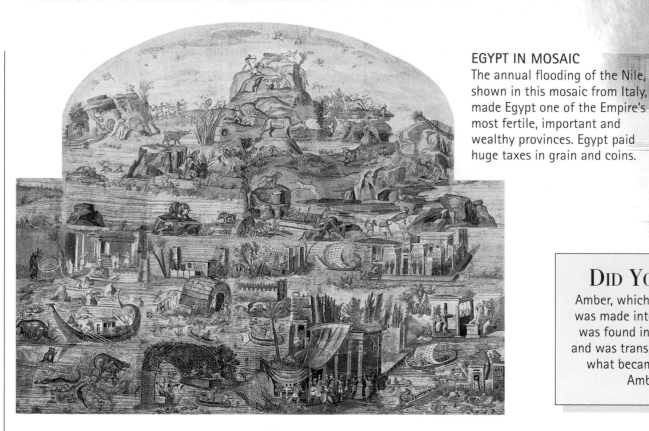

DID YOU KNOW?

Amber, which is fossilised resin, was made into jewellery. Amber was found in the Baltic region and was transported south along what became known as the Amber Road.

CARGO FOR THE CAPITAL
Large trading vessels, equipped with one main sail and often with elaborately carved prows, unloaded at the port of Ostia at the mouth of the River Tiber. The river was too shallow for these ships to travel farther. Smaller boats then took the goods on to Rome.

• EXPANSION AND EMPIRE •

Traders at Home and Abroad

When the Empire expanded, trade increased within Roman boundaries and with countries beyond. Pliny the Younger boasted that "the merchandise of the whole world" could be bought in Rome. Farmers loaded local produce onto bullock wagons (left), mule carts, donkeys and camels and took it to the towns. Spices, perfumes, silk and cotton came from the mysterious East. Road travel, however, was very expensive and only luxury goods were taken over long distances. Shipping was the preferred method of transport, and grain was the most important cargo. Vessels also carried neatly stacked, tall pottery jars, called amphorae. These were filled with wine; fish sauce; and olive oil for lamps, cooking and oiling people's bodies. Merchants could make large fortunes, but they faced high risks of losing cargoes. Roman sailors, who had no navigational instruments, steered across the Mediterranean Sea by looking at the sun, moon and stars. Their wide-hulled, wooden sailing ships were often plundered by pirates or wrecked by storms.

LOADING THE GRAIN
Some tomb paintings pictured people at work. The captain of this boat, named Farnaces, is taking sacks of grain upriver from Ostia to Rome.

THE WILD-ANIMAL TRADE

The ancient Romans enjoyed watching fights between wild beasts, and between wild beasts and gladiators. They imported animals such as tigers (right) from Asia, rhinoceroses from North Africa, wolves from Ireland and bears from Scotland. Towns, such as Leptis Magna in Africa, which specialised in exporting wild animals became very wealthy. During the opening games at the Colosseum in Rome, 9,000 animals died in 100 days. This kind of slaughter wiped out lions in Mesopotamia and elephants in North Africa.

On the March

MILITARY MONUMENT
Soldiers who died in battle were buried with honour. This monument to Gaius Musius, a standard-bearer of the 14th Legion, was erected by his brother.

The conquests of ancient Rome depended on its well-trained army—a powerful fighting force that marched across much of the known world pushing out the Empire's frontiers. At first, only Roman men of property were allowed to serve as soldiers. Then, at the end of the second century BC, General Gaius Marius reformed the army and let citizens without property join. Many poor townsmen signed on for a period of up to 25 years. Military life was tough and punishments were harsh, but when soldiers retired, they were given money or a small plot of land to farm. By Julius Caesar's time, Rome had a highly efficient, wage-earning, permanent army. It was divided into 60 units, or legions, of foot soldiers called legionaries. Augustus later reduced the number of legions to 28 units. Legionaries were supported by auxiliary soldiers who were recruited mostly from the provinces. They formed infantry units (on foot) or cavalry units (on horseback).

MUSEUM PIECES
Many museums in Europe have collections of Roman military equipment. This cavalryman's ceremonial helmet is on display in London's British Museum.

MILITARY EQUIPMENT
A bronze cheek guard (top), an iron spear and javelin head, and the handle from a helmet were found at a fort in England. They were once used by Roman soldiers.

GUARDING THE EMPEROR
The Praetorian Guard, numbering about 9,000 soldiers, was the only part of the army stationed in Rome. Augustus formed this unit to protect the emperor and Italy.

Section of a cohort

THE ROMAN LEGION

A Roman legion consisted of about 5,000 foot soldiers. The legion was divided into nine groups, called cohorts, of equal size, which were led by a tenth, larger cohort. Cohorts were split into six centuries. A century originally contained 100 men, but this number was later reduced to 80 to make the group easier to manage. Centuries were divided into groups of eight soldiers who shared a tent and ate together. Each legion carried a silver eagle into battle. If the eagle fell into enemy hands, the legion was disbanded.

GOING TO WAR
Each group of soldiers, called a century, was commanded by a centurion (front left) and had its own standard-bearer (front centre). Legionaries marched with all their equipment and belongings. Besides their weapons, legionaries carried food for three days and tools for making camp, digging canals, laying roads and building bridges.

DID YOU KNOW?
Regular army pay attracted Rome's poorer citizens into the army. A salt allowance, called a salarium, formed part of a soldier's rations. The English word salary, describing payment of wages, comes from this Latin word "salarium".

RED SLIPWARE
Potteries in Gaul, Italy and Asia Minor produced huge amounts of red tableware. These fine drinking cups show the uniformity of shapes used throughout the Empire.

PORTRAIT OF THE DEAD
When the Romans invaded Egypt, Egyptian artists were influenced by Roman styles. They began to paint more lifelike portraits, such as this, on mummy cases.

• EXPANSION AND EMPIRE •

Growing Empire

Rome's frontiers began to expand long before imperial times. By 264 BC, the Romans dominated the whole of Italy and, after successful wars, ruled the island of Sardinia, territory in Spain and southwest Europe, and Carthage in North Africa. Roman government began in Greece in 146 BC, and during the next century, Rome's boundaries extended to the eastern Mediterranean. In 31 BC, before he became emperor, Augustus finally conquered Egypt. The emperor Claudius overran Mauretania and Thrace, and ordered the invasion of Britain. The emperor Trajan extended the Empire farthest with the conquests of Dacia and large areas of the Middle East. This expansion was later abandoned by his successor Hadrian (above left). Rome divided its territories into provinces, which were governed by senators. Several emperors were born in the provinces. Trajan, for example, came from Spain and Septimius Severus from Africa. Syria and Asia Minor were among Rome's richest provinces, for in those days good crops grew in what is now desert.

HADRIAN'S WALL
The emperor Hadrian ordered the army to build a wall in Britain at the northernmost boundary of Roman territory. Hadrian's Wall, about 120 km (75 miles) long, wound across the country near the present Scottish border. The wall, built mainly between AD 122 and 129, linked 14 forts and was intended to keep out invaders. Parts of the wall still stand.

MILDENHALL TREASURE
This large dish, found at Mildenhall in Suffolk, England, is one of the finest surviving pieces of silverware from ancient Roman times. The central motif represents a sea god. The outer frieze shows followers of Bacchus.

DID YOU KNOW?
The provinces paid taxes to Rome but were not governed by Roman law. Laws, which took account of local customs, were made for each province added to the Empire.

THE PAX ROMANA

From the time of Augustus (left), Roman legions stationed on the frontiers kept the Pax Romana—the peace of Rome. This meant that country people within the borders of the Empire could cultivate their land and raise stock without fear of invasion. The Pax Romana benefited townspeople, too, by protecting trade routes across the Empire. A well-to-do family in Britain, for example, could drink Greek wine from glasses made in Syria and eat from silverware crafted in France.

The Beginnings of Christianity

IN THE ROUND
This mosaic comes from the floor of a Roman villa in Hinton St Mary in Dorset, England. It is the earliest picture of Jesus Christ in Britain.

Jesus, a carpenter by trade, lived in Nazareth, a village in the province of Judaea. When he was 27 or 28 years old, he began preaching to a growing band of followers. These people believed Jesus was chosen by their god to lead them. Some years later, Pontius Pilate, the Roman governor, declared Jesus a rebel against the state and ordered him to be crucified under Roman law. His death inspired the spread of the Christian religion throughout the Empire. Two of Jesus' followers, Peter and Paul, took this new religion to Rome. In its early years, Christianity was very popular with slaves and the poor because it promised everlasting life, regardless of wealth. The Christian belief in one god conflicted with the Roman state religion and with the official view that the emperors were gods. Because Christians would not take part in the ceremonies on special festival days of emperor worship, they were cruelly punished. They were forced to meet secretly.

BEARDED CHRIST
This fourth-century painting is on the ceiling of Commodile Cemetery in Rome. Here, Jesus Christ has a beard as he does in most later Christian art.

GOING UNDERGROUND
When the Romans refused to allow the Christians to bury their dead in official burial places, the Christians dug large passages, called catacombs, beneath uninhabited sections of Rome and Naples, and under some cities in Sicily and North Africa. They placed the shrouded bodies in openings along the walls, which they often decorated with paintings.

CATACOMB PAINTING
Early paintings of Jesus Christ, such as this one on the wall of a catacomb, often showed him as a short-haired, beardless young man in the role of the Good Shepherd.

TOMB INSCRIPTION
This inscription from Rome's catacombs dates from the third century. It is simpler than most tomb inscriptions and may have been carved secretly and in haste.

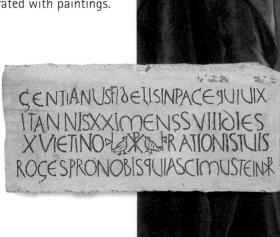

THE EDICT OF MILAN

Christianity soon attracted followers both rich and poor. It spread so rapidly that by 311 the emperor Galerius passed a law allowing Christians to worship openly "on condition they in no way act against the established order". Two years later, the Edict of Milan issued by the emperor Constantine I gave Christians the freedom to inherit and dispose of property, and to elect their own church government. Constantine I (above) was baptised as a Christian shortly before he died in 337. In 380, under Theodosius I, Christianity became the official religion of the Empire.

THE GOOD SHEPHERD
This fine statue of Jesus Christ as the Good Shepherd is remarkable because it was made in secret at a time when Christianity was still generally forbidden.

BATTLING THE BARBARIANS
Scenes from battles were often
carved on large stone coffins, known
as sarcophagi. This one belonged to a
general who fought in the Germanic
wars in Marcus Aurelius's army.

DID YOU KNOW?

Diocletian sent out officials to count
the Empire's population. They brought
back detailed information. The census
counted everything from people to
livestock and olive trees.

Empire in Decline

The huge Roman Empire was difficult and expensive
to run. From AD 161 to 180, the emperor Marcus
Aurelius had to fight many campaigns to protect the
boundaries. By the third century AD, the army was stretched
too far and taxes were raised to cover the Empire's costs.
Farmers who could not afford the taxes abandoned their farms, and
cities suffered as the economy slumped and their markets declined.
Many emperors were weak, so generals competed for power. Civil
wars raged, and barbarians, sensing the Empire's weakness, attacked
the frontiers. Diocletian (above left) became emperor in AD 284.
He split the Empire in order to make it easier to manage, appointing
Maximian to rule the West, and keeping the wealthier East for
himself. Diocletian also reorganised the army and the provinces.
Soon after Diocletian and Maximian retired in 305, civil wars broke
out again until Constantine took power over the whole Empire
in 324. He moved the imperial court to Byzantium, which he
renamed Constantinople.

TRIUMPHAL ARCH

The Arch of Constantine was built to celebrate a victory at the Battle of the Milvian Bridge near Rome in 312. Many of the arch's best carvings were stolen from second-century monuments.

COLLECTING TAXES

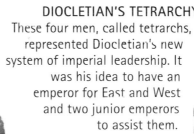

Emperors needed huge sums of money to support the large army and pay for their extravagant lifestyles, expensive works of art, large building programs and the corn dole. This revenue was raised through taxation. People had to pay taxes on land, slaves, crops, roads and goods from shops. Tax officials (above) were required to collect set amounts of money and had to make up any shortfall from their own wages. They were harsh and unfeeling about collecting what was owed.

DIOCLETIAN'S TETRARCHY

These four men, called tetrarchs, represented Diocletian's new system of imperial leadership. It was his idea to have an emperor for East and West and two junior emperors to assist them.

ATTILA THE HUN

The Huns were a barbarian tribe from central Asia. By 447, Attila, king of the Huns, and his large army of warriors had conquered all the countries between the Black Sea and the Mediterranean. They defeated the Roman army in three battles, but did not capture Constantinople and Rome.

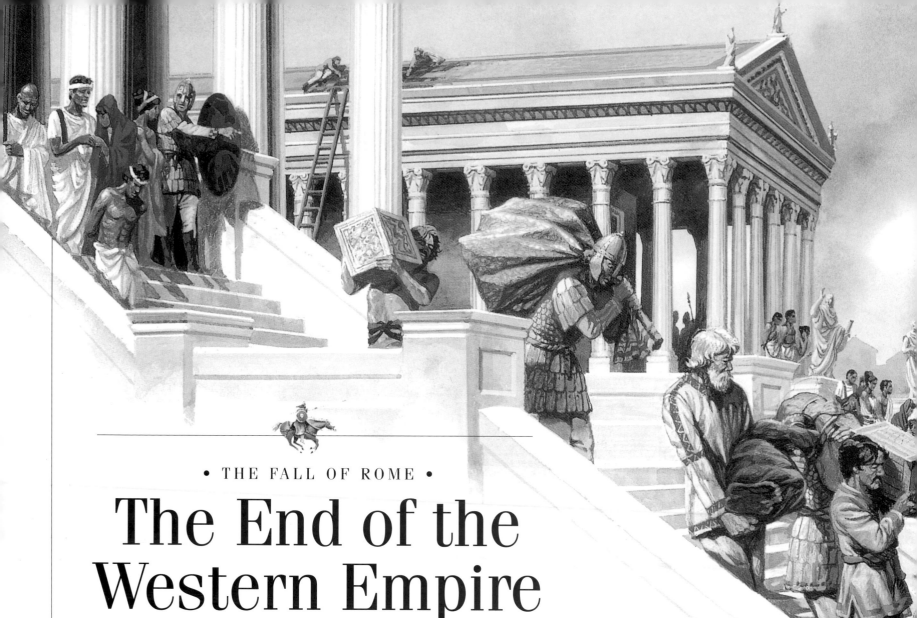

The End of the Western Empire

The Romans, like the ancient Greeks, called all tribes whose language they could not understand "barbarians". The emperor Theodosius I allowed German barbarian tribes to settle in the north of the Empire when they were driven there by the fierce Asiatic Huns. But by the early fifth century, other barbarian people, including the Huns themselves, came looking for land to settle. They fought the imperial armies and the Germans, and soon occupied large areas that had once been Roman territory. After Theodosius I died in 395, the Western and Eastern Roman empires split forever in matters of government, but the West still depended upon the East for money and grain supplies. King Alaric led the Visigoths into Rome in 410 and became the first person to conquer the city in 800 years. The Vandals later plundered Rome in 455. The Eastern Empire refused to help the Western Empire, which finally ended in 476 when the last Western emperor, Romulus Augustulus, was exiled by the barbarians.

SACKING OF ROME
Gaiseric, leader of the barbarian Vandals, sailed to Ostia in AD 455. His soldiers entered Rome and spent 12 days stripping buildings of everything valuable, including the gilded roof tiles of important temples. Gaiseric took the widow of the emperor Valentinian III and her daughters hostage.

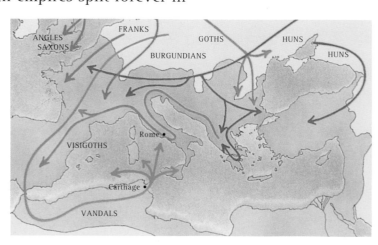

BESET BY BARBARIANS
Hordes of barbarians seeking land attacked the frontiers and swarmed into the Western Empire.

VILLAS FOR VANDALS
When the Vandals overran Roman territory in North Africa, local landowners faced slavery or exile. This mosaic from Carthage shows a Vandal in front of a Roman villa.

SAFE HARBOUR
Ravenna became the Western Empire's capital in 402. The city was connected to the mainland by a causeway. Ships entering the harbour had to pass between lighthouse towers.

SPREADING CHRISTIANITY

The Christian Church survived when the Western Empire collapsed and Rome became the holiest of Western Christian cities. The first Christian monasteries were in Egypt, but soon monastic communities were formed throughout the former Western Empire. The monks preserved many ancient Roman manuscripts by patiently copying them out by hand. The symbol at right, called a Chi-Rho, was one of the earliest Christian symbols and is found on many Christian objects. It combines the first two letters of Christ's name in Greek.

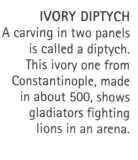

IVORY DIPTYCH
A carving in two panels is called a diptych. This ivory one from Constantinople, made in about 500, shows gladiators fighting lions in an arena.

PANEL PICTURE
The Byzantine Christians produced panel pictures called icons. They were often painted on wood, like this one of St Gregory.

SIGN OF VICTORY
Before winning the Battle of the Milvian Bridge, Constantine I claimed he saw a flaming cross and the words "In this conquer". The cross became a Christian symbol.

• THE FALL OF ROME •

Eastern Empire

The Empire in the East, which came to be known as the Byzantine Empire, prospered as the Western Empire weakened. The city of Constantinople grew wealthy. Its geographical position between Europe and Asia was good both for trade and for managing its territory. The frontiers of the Byzantine Empire extended west to Greece, south to Egypt, and east to the border with Arabia. Although Greek was the official language of the East, Latin was often still spoken at the emperor's court. During his rule from 527 to 565, Justinian (above left) regained some of the western provinces in Africa, Italy and Spain, but he did not hold them for long. Many other Eastern emperors had long reigns and governed well. The Byzantine Empire was never a great military power and tried to settle difficulties with its neighbours by peaceful means. Its people were Christians, and invaders who threatened the Empire were frequently persuaded to join it instead and become Christians, too.

50

EASTERN CAPITAL

Like Rome, Constantinople (left) covered seven hills. The emperor Constantine I began a grand building program to beautify Constantinople, which was protected by water on three sides. Later, a wall was built around the city by Theodosius II. Justinian I built Hagia Sophia, which was the largest Christian church of the time.

OTTOMAN TURKS

During the thirteenth century, the Ottoman Empire, which was located in what is now Turkey, began to expand its frontiers. The Ottoman Turks followed the Islamic religion and set out to conquer Christian cities. Gradually they controlled most of the Eastern Roman Empire. The troops of Sultan Mehmet II (above) besieged Constantinople for six weeks before the city finally fell in 1453. This was the end of the Byzantine Empire and Constantinople became known as Istanbul.

GOLDEN GIFT

The empress Theodora, Justinian's wife, was very generous to the Christian Church. Here, attended by her ladies-in-waiting, she presents a golden chalice to the Church of San Vitale in Ravenna, Italy.

NEARBY TOWN

The town of Herculaneum was also buried by the eruption of Mt Vesuvius. Many people fled through these streets to shelter in the boat storage chambers beside the beach. Their skeletons were discovered in 1982.

DID YOU KNOW?

The people of Pompeii and Herculaneum were completely unprepared for the eruption of Vesuvius in AD 79. They did not even know they were living beside an active volcano until that fateful day in August.

• THE FALL OF ROME •

Discovering Ancient Rome

The Roman Empire was one of the largest the world has ever known. Many of its structures still stand and they tell us about Roman architectural styles, building methods and materials, and town planning. Remains of frontier fortifications, aqueducts and roads show the extent of this great civilisation. Surviving art and collections of objects once in daily use help us form a picture of the Roman people. We also know a lot about their hopes, ambitions and feelings from inscriptions on stone and metal, and from the many surviving copies of original histories, poems, plays, scientific works, recipe books, letters and official lists. The Latin alphabet, expanded from 22 to 26 letters, is used today throughout the Western world. Latin shaped the languages of modern Italy, France, Spain, Portugal and Romania. Many English words also come from Latin. Scientists, doctors and lawyers still use Latin phrases, and every known species of plant and animal has a Latin name.

NO PROTECTION

Many of Pompeii's victims died with their arms raised above their heads. People tried to cover their heads with their cloaks as the fiery ash rained down upon them.

GUARD DOG

This plaster model shows how a watchdog outside the House of Vesonius Primus in Pompeii died during the eruption. He was chained up and could not flee from the ash.

52

FROZEN IN TIME
When Mt Vesuvius in southern Italy erupted in AD 79, Pompeii was buried under 3 m (10 ft) of boiling ash and lapilli in only a few hours. Archaeologists have been uncovering the city since 1748. The remains of streets, shops, villas and gardens were well preserved beneath the ash.

WALL PAINTING
Many paintings in Pompeii were preserved because they were buried. Some fine frescoes survive, such as this one dating from the second century BC in the Villa of the Mysteries.

ABANDONED MEAL
When Mt Vesuvius erupted, the terrified people ran from their homes. The food being cooked in these pots at the House of Vettii was never served.

BEWARE OF THE DOG
In one Pompeii house, a realistic floor mosaic took the place of a real guard dog. The words "cave canem" mean "beware of the dog".

RECORDING THE PAST
Edward Gibbon was an English historian who thought history should record "the crimes, follies and misfortunes of mankind". When he visited Rome in 1764, he decided to write *The History of the Decline and Fall of the Roman Empire.* This work, which is still read, covered the years from the destruction of the Western Empire to the end of the Eastern Empire. Gibbon read documents from the ancient world, and studied maps, coins and ruins to support his account of ancient Rome. The first volume was published in 1776; the sixth in 1788.

Discover more in Growing Empire

Tributes to the Emperors

When Augustus, the first emperor, died in AD 14, the Roman Senate declared him a god. From then onward, people worshipped the emperors, and temples were dedicated to them all over the Empire. These impressive buildings reminded everyone of the emperors' absolute power. Monuments erected to celebrate victories in war also helped to advertise the strength of rulers. Emperors issued coins bearing their images, and commissioned paintings, mosaics and sculptures of themselves and their families. The style and symbolism of imperial portraits often tell us more about the way an emperor wished his subjects to see him rather than giving us a true likeness. Some of the most important emperors are listed below.

Augustus

Augustus	27 BC–AD 14	Philip	244–249	**DIVISION OF THE ROMAN EMPIRE** AD 395	
Tiberius	14–37	Decius	249–251		
Caligula	37–41	Trebonianus Gallus	251–253	**WESTERN EMPIRE**	
Claudius I	41–54			Honorius	394–423
Nero	54–68	Aemilianus	253	Valentinian III	423–455
Galba	68–69	Valerian I	253–259	Maximus	455
Otho	69	Gallienus	259–268	Avitus	455–456
Vitellius	69	Claudius II	268–270	Majorian	457–461
Vespasian	69–79	Quintillus	270	Severus	461–465
Titus	79–81	Aurelian	270–275	Anthemius	467–472
Domitian	81–96	Tacitus	275–276	Olybrius	472
Nerva	96–98	Florianus	276	Glycerius	473–474
Trajan	98–117	Probus	276–282	Nepos	474–475
Hadrian	117–138	Carus	282–283	Romulus Augustulus	475–476
Antoninus Pius	138–161	Carinus	283–285		
Marcus Aurelius	161–180	Diocletian	284–305		
Commodus	180–192	Maximian	286–305	**EASTERN EMPIRE**	
Pertinax	193	Constantine and Licinius	307	Arcadius	395–408
Didius Julianus	193			Theodosius II	408–450
Septimius Severus	193–211	Constantine I	324–337	Marcian	450–457
		Constantine II	337–340	Leo I	457–474
Caracalla	211–217	Constans	340–350	Zeno	474–491
Macrinus	217–218	Constantius	340–361	Anastasius I	491–518
Elagabalus	218–222	Julian	361–363	Justin I	518–527
Severus Alexander	222–235	Jovian	363–364	Justinian I	527–565
		Valentinian I	364–375		
Maximinus	235–238	Valens	364–378		
Gordian I	238	Gratian	378–383		
Gordian II	238	Valentinian II	375–392		
Gordian III	238–244	Theodosius I	379–395		

MESSAGES FROM STATUES
Augustus (above) appears as a godlike hero. His breastplate symbolises military successes and the boy-god Cupid links the emperor with Venus, the goddess of love. Caligula (below) assumes a commanding pose on horseback.

Caligula

PORTRAITS OF EMPERORS
Portrait busts of new emperors were sent to the provinces so their subjects could have some idea of what the ruler looked like. Although many emperors travelled widely, they could not visit every part of the Empire.

EMPEROR ON HORSEBACK
This bronze statue of Marcus Aurelius, designed to inspire his subjects, shows him as a forceful soldier. In his writings, however, he comes across as a quiet, thoughtful student of philosophy.

Marcus Aurelius

Caracalla

Nero

Hadrian

Trajan

Valerian I

Constantine I

Honorius

Romulus Augustulus

IMPERIAL COINAGE
A portrait of the emperor of the time adorned one side of imperial coins, which were made of gold, silver or bronze. Images on coins were an excellent way to make sure that people in the provinces knew the emperor's face.

Index

Picture Credits

(t=top, b=bottom, l=left, r=right, c=centre, F=front, C=cover, B=back, Bg=background)
AKG London, 20cl (E. Lessing/Museo Ostiense). Ancient Art & Architecture Collection, 6br, 13br, 20tc, 22tl, 34bl, 40tl, 51br, 52br, 53bl, 54br (R. Sheridan). Peter Arnold Inc., 25br (J.L. Amos), 15b (M. Cooper). Austral International, 52/53c (Pictor Uniphoto). The Bridgeman Art Library, 18tl (Archaelogical Museum, Naples), 19cl, 25bl, 34tr, 49tr (The British Museum), 44tl (Dorset County Museum), 10tl (Giraudon), 11bl (Kunsthistorisches Museum, Vienna), 17tl (Lauros-Giraudon), 40c (Louvre, Paris), 14bl, 22bl (Metropolitan Museum of Modern Art, New York), 50tl (Pushkin Museum, Moscow), 12cr (Villa dei Misteri, Pompei), 46tr, 55tr, 55bcr, 55br. The British Museum, 10bl, 14cr, 15cr, 19tc, 21tr, 25c, 30bl, 42tl, 42bl. Bulloz, 12tr. C.M. Dixon, 18cl (The British Museum), 19tr, 19br, 25bc, (Capitoline Museum, Rome), 50tr (Heritage Museum, Leningrad), 36tl (National Architecture Museum, Naples), 16tl, 38br, 44br, 45br, 55bc (Vatican Museums), 6bl, 8bl, 16tr, 20bc, 20bcl, 20tl, 28tl, 31tr, 31cl, 32tcl, 32bcl, 40tr, 50bl, 53tl, 52bl. Michael Freeman, 19cr (Intl. Perfume Museum, Grasse), 40cl, 42cl. The Granger Collection, 28tr, 53br. Sonia Halliday

Photographs, 44cl (A. Held), 37tl, 39tr. Robert Harding Picture Library, 40cr (The British Museum), 28cl (Rado Museum, Tunis), 37tr (E. Rooney), 45tr (P. Scholey), 26bc, 43tl. Jurgen Liepe, 42tr. Nasjonalgalleriet, Oslo, 17cr (J. Lathion/Ethnological Museum, Oslo). Reunion des Musees Nationaux, 16bl (Louvre, Paris). Scala, 28bc (Arcivescovado, Ravenna), 12cl, 53cr (Casa dei Vetti, Pompei), 8tr (Cortona, Museo dell'Accademia Etrusca), 55tcl (Galleria degli Uffizi, Firenze), 11br, 19bl, 24bc, 35tr (Musei Capitolini, Roma), 25tr (Museo Archeologico, Adria), 26bl, 26c (Museo Archeologico, Aquileia), 8tl (Museo Archeologico, Firenze), 38tl (Museo Archeologico, Palestrina) 34tl (Museo Archeologico, Taranto), 23b (Museo Archeologico, Venezia), 50c (Museo Benaki, Athenai) 8bc (Museo Civico Piacenza), 36c (Museo della Civilta' Romana, Roma), 46tl (Museo delle Terme, Roma), 8cr (Museo di Villa Giulia, Roma), 8br (Museo Gregoriano Etrusco, Vaticano), 32tr, 34tl, 34bc, (Museo Gregoriano Profano, Vaticano), 31br (Museo Nazionale Atestino, Este), 14cl, 22tr, 24tl, 32bl, 32cr, 33br, 34cl, (Museo Nazionale, Napoli), 12bl, 55tc (Museo Pio-Clementino, Vaticano), 49tl (S. Apollinare Nuovo, Ravenna), 3, 14tl, (Villa dei Misteri, Pompei), 30tl (Villa Romana del Casale, Piazza Armerina), 1, 8/9r, 10br, 12br, 38bl, 44bl, 45tl, 45r, 52tl, 54tr, 55bl, 55bcl, Werner Forman Archive, 55tcr (Barber Institute of Fine

Arts, Birmingham University), 51tr (Topkapi Palace Library, Istanbul), 17c (Scavi di Ostia), 53tr.

Illustration Credits

Paul Bachem, 4/5b, 5tl, 28/29c, 28bl, 36/37c, 42/43c. Kenn Backhaus, 5br, 6/7c, 12/13c, 50/51c. Chris Forsey, 4b, 20/21c, 34/35c. Ray Grinaway, 40/41c, 40bl. Adam Hook/Bernard Thornton Artists, UK, 18/19c, 38/39c. Janet Jones, 2, 16/17c, 32/33c. Iain McKellar, 22/23c. Peter Mennim, 14/15c, 30/31c. Matthew Ottley, 46/47b. John Richards, 48/49c, 48br. Ken Rinkel, 40br. Sharif Tarabay/Garden Studio, 4tl, 5tr, 24/25c, 44/45c. Rod Westblade, endpapers, icons. Ann Winterbotham, 4cl, 5bc, 10/11c, 26/27c, 26tl.

Cover Credits

Ray Grinaway, FCb. Nasjonalgalleriet, Oslo, FCtl (J. Lathion/Ethnographical Museum, Oslo). Scala, Bg (Museo Gregoriano Profano, Vaticano).